LET'S VISIT ETHIOPIA

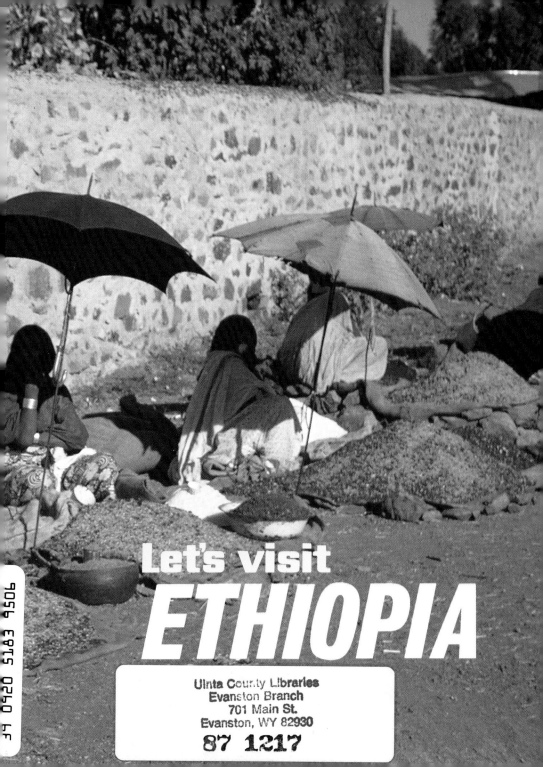

Let's visit
ETHIOPIA

First published 1984
© Richard Pankhurst 1984

ACKNOWLEDGEMENTS

The Author and Publishers are grateful to the following for permission to reproduce copyright photographs in this book:

Art Directors Photo Library, The British Library, Colorific Photo Library, Eugénie Peter.

CIP data
Pankhurst, Richard
    Let's visit Ethiopia.
    1. Ethiopia – Social life and customs – Juvenile literature
    I. Title
    963'.06   DT379.5
ISBN 0 222 00965 9

Burke Publishing Company Limited
Pegasus House, 116–120 Golden Lane, London EC1Y 0TL, England.
Burke Publishing (Canada) Limited
Registered Office: 20 Queen Street West, Suite 3000, Box 30, Toronto, Canada M5H 1V5.
Burke Publishing Company Inc.
Registered Office: 333 State Street, PO Box 1740, Bridgeport, Connecticut 06601, U.S.A.
Typeset in "Monophoto" Baskerville by Green Gates Studios Ltd.
Printed in Singapore by Tien Wah Press (Pte) Ltd.

Contents

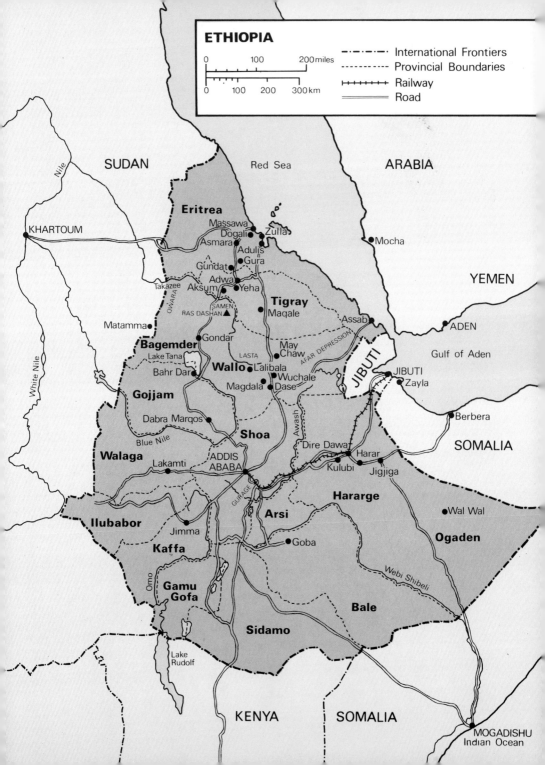

ETHIOPIA

0   100   200 miles
0   100   200   300 km

—·—·—·— International Frontiers
- - - - - - Provincial Boundaries
+++++++ Railway
——— Road

SUDAN

Red Sea

ARABIA

KHARTOUM

Nile

Eritrea

Massawa
Dogali   Zulla
Asmara
Adulis
Gura
Gundat
Adwa
Aksum   Yeha
Takazee
OQARA
SAMEN
RAS DASHAN ▲
Tigray
Maqale

Mocha

YEMEN

ADEN

Assab

Gulf of Aden

White Nile

Matamma

Bagemder
Gondar
Lake Tana
LASTA
Wallo   Lalibala
Bahr Dar
May
Chaw
AFAR DEPRESSION

JIBUTI

JIBUTI
Zayla

Gojjam
Magdala   Wuchale
Dase
Dabra Marqos
Blue Nile
Shoa
Awash

Berbera

SOMALIA

Walaga
Lakamti
**ADDIS
ABABA**
GURAGE

Dire Dawar
Harar
Kulubi   Jigjiga

Ilubabor
Jimma
Kaffa
Arsi
Goba

Hararge

Wal Wal

Ogaden

**Gamu
Gofa**
Omo

Webi Shibeli

Bale

Lake
Rudolf

Sidamo

KENYA   SOMALIA

MOGADISHU
Indian Ocean

Let's Visit Ethiopia

Ethiopia is a largely isolated country situated in the north-eastern corner of Africa where one of the two branches of the River Nile has its source. It has long fascinated the outside world. Converted to Christianity in the early fourth century, Ethiopia is one of the oldest Christian countries. In the Middle Ages it was regarded with awe in the West as the only Christian kingdom outside Europe. For a long time it was thought to be a mysterious land ruled by a fabulous priest-king called Prester John. The far-off realm later attracted the interest of Ignatius Loyola, founder of the Order of Jesuits. In the seventeenth century several Jesuit missionaries attempted, unsuccessfully, to bring Ethiopia under the control of the Pope in Rome. In the eighteenth century, the country aroused new interest in Europe when Samuel Johnson, author of the famous English Dictionary, made it the subject of his widely-read novel *Rasselas*. Later in the same century, the great Scottish explorer James Bruce travelled to Ethiopia to discover the source of the Blue Nile, and wrote a five-volume book about the still little-known land, its people and their history.

This ancient African state succeeded in preserving its independence throughout the nineteenth century. This was the period of imperialism which witnessed the European "Scramble

The Blue Nile Falls

for Africa", when European colonies and protectorates were established throughout the African continent. The Italians attempted to establish a protectorate over Ethiopia in the 1890s, but Emperor Menilek, one of the greatest rulers the country ever produced, defeated them decisively at the Battle of Adwa in 1896—the most resounding victory of an African army over a European army since the time of Hannibal. As a result, Ethiopia remained free from foreign rule. By the end of the century, it was the only remaining independent African state.

Ethiopia, which had joined the League of Nations in 1923, was the first country to be invaded by a fascist power in the years leading up to the Second World War. Mussolini's Italy, acting entirely without provocation, invaded Ethiopia in 1935. The invasion of an almost defenceless country led to considerable international indignation. The League of Nations condemned Italy as the aggressor, and imposed economic sanctions against her. This meant that all members of the League were requested to stop trading with Italy, lending her money, or selling her weapons. These steps, however, failed to halt the aggression. After eight months of fierce fighting the Italians, who had vastly superior weapons and who made considerable use of aerial bombing and poison-gas, succeeded in capturing the Ethiopian capital, Addis Ababa. The emperor, Haile Selassie, fled from his country. He went to

Massawa: the memorial to Menilek's victory at Adwa in 1896

address the League of Nations in Geneva, and then spent the next few years as an exile in Britain.

Meanwhile Mussolini proclaimed the creation of a new "Roman Empire" in Africa. Many Ethiopians, taking advantage of their mountainous countryside, nevertheless continued to resist the Italians for the next four years. They did so entirely without help from outside.

Mussolini's entry into the European War in 1940 brought about a rapid change in East Africa. Britain, which was by then fighting almost alone, considered the Red Sea of major strategic importance, because it lay on the main route to India and the East. The British were therefore anxious to destroy fascist power in East Africa. For this reason the Ethiopian patriots, who had never surrendered to the Italians, were seen as useful allies. British officers were flown into Ethiopia to encourage the patriots, and a liberation campaign was launched early in 1941. The Italian empire rapidly crumbled. Ethiopia, the first victim of fascist aggression, became the first to be freed from fascist rule. Haile Selassie returned to his throne in triumph. He was to rule for another three decades, but was then deposed after the Ethiopian Revolution of 1974.

Because of its long history of independence—interrupted only by five years of Italian occupation—Ethiopia has enjoyed a special position in Africa, and in African political and diplomatic affairs. After the Second World War, Addis Ababa was chosen as the headquarters of Africa's two principal organisations: the Organisation of African Unity (O.A.U.)

10

Addis Ababa: Stained glass windows in Africa Hall

and the United Nations' Economic Commission for Africa (E.C.A.). The latter is housed in Africa Hall, a fine modern building with beautiful stained-glass windows designed by Afewerk Tekle, Ethiopia's foremost artist.

Ethiopia has been deeply influenced by its history. Today it is one of the largest and most populous, as well as one of the most important, countries in Africa; and it is different in many ways from any other territory on that continent.

The Ethiopians, many of whom speak Semitic languages related to Hebrew and Arabic, are the only people in Africa to have their own form of writing. This script, which dates back at least two thousand years, has its origin in the old Sabaean writing developed several thousands of years ago in south Arabia.

The Ethiopians also have their own special calendar, which was borrowed from ancient Egypt. This calendar has twelve equal months, each of thirteen days, together with a short additional, or "thirteenth", month of five days (or six in leap-years). Ethiopians often therefore boast that their country enjoys thirteen months of sunshine. The year in Ethiopia begins, not at the beginning of January, but in the second week of our September. The Ethiopian year is, moreover, seven years behind ours until the end of our December after which it becomes eight years behind. (Christmas in Ethiopia is celebrated, as in some other eastern Christian lands, on January 7th.)

The Ethiopians also reckon the hours of the day in a different way. Like many peoples of Africa and the Middle East they consider that the day begins at dawn. Because they live near the Equator, dawn takes place at roughly the same time throughout the year, without much change between summer and winter. Mid-day is thus spoken of in Ethiopia not as "twelve o'clock", but as "six o'clock".

This country was little known to the outside world until recently. Its history and civilisation are unique in many ways.

The Country

Ethiopia has also been known abroad during part of its history as Abyssinia.

The term Ethiopia comes from the Greek word for "burnt face", and was the name given by the ancient Greeks to the Ethiopians (and other peoples south of Egypt) because their complexion was darker than that of other nations with whom the Greeks were familiar. From the time of their conversion to Christianity in the early part of the fourth century, the Ethiopians were proud of the name Ethiopia, for the Bible contains several complimentary references to it.

The term Abyssinia is, on the other hand, of Arabic origin. It comes from the Arabic *Habash*. This was the name of one of the first Ethiopian tribes with whom the Arabs made contact, and it was therefore the name they gave to the country as a whole. However, it can also be interpreted in Arabic as meaning "mixed" and the Ethiopians therefore tended to consider it as having a derogatory meaning. The name Abyssinia was, nevertheless, adopted in most European languages for many years.

The Ethiopians themselves have always called their country Ethiopia. This is the name by which it is generally known today.

13

In the Gondar market

Ethiopia is the seventh largest country in all Africa—almost as large as France and Spain combined. In North American terms, it covers an area comparable to Texas, Oklahoma and New Mexico.

The country is roughly the shape of a triangle or pyramid. Its base rests on the northern border of Kenya and part of Somalia. To the west of Ethiopia lies the Sudan, and to the east (from north to south) are the Red Sea, the tiny country of Jibuti, and Somalia.

Because of its vast size Ethiopia is a land of immense contrasts. About two-thirds of the country rises high above the low-lying coastal belt. The highlands are mainly between

14

1,800 and 3,500 metres (6,000 and 10,000 feet) above the level of the sea. There are also numerous high mountains and deep ravines. The tallest mountain, Ras Dashan, towers 4,500 metres (15,000 feet) above sea level. On the other hand, there are also extensive lowlands, mainly in the east, south and west; and part of the Danakil depression in the north-east actually drops below sea level. Another important geographical feature is the Rift Valley, which runs right across the centre of the country from north-east to south-west. The Rift Valley is the northernmost section of the Great African Rift—a geological depression which extends from the Jordan Valley southwards across Africa to Mozambique.

Near the gorge of the Blue Nile

The principal rivers include the Blue Nile and its northern tributary, the Takazee, and the Awash which is remarkable in that it loses itself in the Danakil depression without ever reaching the sea. Far away in the south, there are two other sizeable rivers, the Omo and the Webi Shebeli, which flow into Lake Rudolf and Somalia respectively. These and most other Ethiopian rivers differ from rivers in many other countries in that they hamper communication rather than make it easier.

For most of the year, Ethiopian rivers do not contain enough water to allow boats to float in them. This is partly because the rain falls during a particular season of the year only, and partly because much of the rain which does fall evaporates. During the rains, however, the river currents are too fast for safe navigation. In addition, most Ethiopian settlements are

A salt lake in the Danakil depression

River transport

situated in mountainous areas. These areas are far healthier than the land close to rivers where malaria is a common disease. For all these reasons, the rivers of Ethiopia for the most part make no effective contribution to inter-town or long-distance traffic through the country.

The great variations in altitude in Ethiopia have resulted in equally immense contrasts in climate. The highlands enjoy almost perfect weather. Although they are situated within a few degrees of the Equator, they are never too hot; in fact, at night they can be quite cold. In the higher mountain areas, the night temperature often falls below freezing-point, and snow can sometimes be seen on the peaks of Ras Dashan. The lowlands, on the other hand, tend to have a torrid climate, while the Red Sea ports of Massawa and Assab are among the hottest places in the world.

17

A straw-roofed home and storage hut in the fertile west of Ethiopia

Much of the highland region is extremely fertile, with deep soil and abundant rainfall. In these areas there are two rainy seasons: a major one from mid-June to mid-September, and a smaller and less regular one between February and May. Large areas in the north are seriously eroded.

The lowlands, by contrast, suffer from scant rainfall. They consist in the main of scrublands; but, in some places, they are virtual deserts. Thickly wooded forests are nevertheless to be found in the south-west. In the rest of the country trees are scarce, although eucalyptus, which were first imported at the

18

end of the nineteenth century by Emperor Menilek, have been planted in and around Addis Ababa and the other principal settlements and even in many villages. When driving, one's first sight of a town is thus often the dark slender trees of its eucalyptus forest.

Transport in so large and mountainous a country has always presented major difficulties. A road network was begun early in the twentieth century, expanded during the Italian fascist occupation, and further developed (with World Bank assistance) after the liberation. All-weather roads now link the capital with the principal towns. There are also many dry-season tracks—a large proportion of them constructed after the Ethiopian Revolution by local communities. Much of the population nevertheless still lives in areas which are virtually inaccessible by road.

Besides the road network there is a single railway line, built as a result of a concession granted by Emperor Menilek at the end of the nineteenth century. This line runs from Addis Ababa via the railway town of Dire Dawa to the port of Jibuti on the Gulf of Aden.

In recent years, the development of civil aviation has made transport and communications much easier. There are fine airports in Ethiopia capable of handling modern jet planes. They are located at Addis Ababa, Asmara, Assab and Dire Dawa. There are also a large number of smaller landing-strips throughout the country. Ethiopian Airlines, which is recognised as one of the finest airlines in Africa, makes regular

The palace at Massawa

flights to numerous international capitals, including London, Frankfurt, Rome, New Delhi and Peking.

The country has a coastline, on the Red Sea, of no less than 1,280 kilometres (800 miles), and two well-equipped ports: Massawa, an old town dating back to early medieval times, and Assab which became economically important only after the Second World War. These two ports, together with Jibuti, handle the bulk of Ethiopia's import-export trade; and because they are within easy reach of the southern Red Sea, they are also of major tourist interest.

The People

Ethiopia, which is thought to have a population of no less than forty million, is inhabited by many distinct peoples. Because of the country's rugged terrain, they have until recently remained fairly isolated from each other. They speak entirely different—though in some cases related—languages, and have many different customs and traditions.

Most of the languages spoken in Ethiopia belong to two main families: the Semitic and the Hamitic.

The Semitic languages, which are related to Hebrew and Arabic, are mainly spoken in the north and centre of the country, but are also found in small pockets in the south and east. Five Semitic languages are spoken in Ethiopia today and they all derive from the old classical language Ge'ez. Ge'ez is sometimes called the "Latin of Ethiopia", as the other Semitic languages of Ethiopia derive from Ge'ez, just as French, Italian, Romanian and the other Romance languages of Europe derive from Latin. Ge'ez is also the language into which the Ethiopian Bible was first translated, and the one in which all old Ethiopian literature is written. Although it is now largely a "dead" language which is no longer used in everyday speech, it is still used in church services and in church poetry, or *qene*, which is still being composed to this day. The

21

An Ethiopian priest with a medieval Bible. The illustrations are hand-painted

principal living Semitic languages in Ethiopia are Tigrinya, which is spoken throughout the province of Tigray, as well as in the central highlands of Eritrea; Tigre, which is used in some parts of western and eastern Eritrea; Amharic, originally the tongue of north-western and central Ethiopia and today the official language of the State as well as the language of modern literature; Gurage, spoken by people of that name who live to the south of Addis Ababa; and Harari, or Adare, a language which is remarkable in being known only by the inhabitants of a single town, the old walled city of Harar.

The Hamitic languages (unlike the Semitic) are found

mainly in Ethiopia. They have some similarity with the latter but are only loosely related to them. They are spoken mainly in the south, but also in a few small areas of the north. The principal members of this language family are Beja, which is used in western Eritrea; Saho, further to the east; Afar, in the north-east of the country; Somali in the south-east; and, by far the most widely used, Oromo (sometimes called Galla), the language of much of the southern and central parts of the country. The three latter languages are also spoken in neighbouring countries: Afar in northern Jibuti, Somali in southern Jibuti and the whole of Somalia, and Oromo in northern Kenya. There are also several other groups of languages in

A street in the old walled city of Harar

Ethiopia, notably the Omotic languages, spoken far away in the south-west; and the Nilo-Saharan languages, used along the border with the Sudan.

Though Ethiopia has long been renowned as one of the oldest Christian countries, it is also inhabited by followers of two other major religions: Islam and Judaism, as well as by spirit-worshippers who were formerly known as Pagans.

Christianity, which is the most important of the religions in Ethiopia, may well have first arrived in the country at the time of the Apostles. Christianity became the state religion of the Aksumite Kingdom in the early fourth century, and later expanded widely throughout the northern and central highlands. The Ethiopian church was associated with the Coptic church of Egypt for over one thousand years, and therefore has much in common with other Orthodox and Eastern churches, namely those of the Copts, Greeks, Syrians, Armenians and South Indians. Christianity was the official religion of the country until the Ethiopian Revolution in 1974, when a secular state (with no official religion) was established. Since that time, however, many new churches have been built, and church-going has, in fact, greatly increased in recent years. Many Ethiopians travel each year in December to worship at the church of St. Gabriel at Kulubi, near Harar. This is renowned as a place of pilgrimage and people come here to pray, make vows and ask God to grant them children, good health and other blessings.

In addition to the members of the Ethiopian church, there are several thousand Catholics, Lutherans and Adventists in Ethiopia, mainly in the towns. They have been converted by European and American missionaries. Foreign missions operate in several parts of the country and they are often active in the fields of education and health.

Islam, the second of the major religions in Ethiopia, made its first appearance at the time of the Prophet Muhammad, several of whose earliest followers found refuge at Aksum. Their faith has many adherents in modern Ethiopia, particularly towards the east, south and west of the country.

Judaism is represented in Ethiopia by the Falashas—sometimes referred to as the Black Jews of Africa. Their ancestors are thought to have come to the country in ancient times, from

The Mosque in Asmara

Egypt or Arabia, and to have succeeded in converting a sizeable part of the population. However, their influence later declined greatly, and today they number no more than fifteen thousand. After the Second World War, many Falashas developed close ties with Jewish communities abroad. A number went to Israel, after 1948, for religious and other studies. On returning home, they introduced Hebrew (the traditional language of prayer for the Jews) into Falasha religious services. (Until that time the Falashas worshipped, like the Ethiopian Christians, solely in the Ge'ez language.)

26

There has also been a considerable amount of Falasha emigration in recent years, both to Israel and elsewhere.

Farming is a major occupation in Ethiopia. Although there are a number of mechanised farms, all of them today under State ownership, some of the methods used by Ethiopian farmers have remained unchanged for centuries. In the neighbourhood of some of the lakes and rivers live hunters and food-gatherers whose methods and way of life are similar to those of early man in other parts of the world. The arid scrub-lands are inhabited by nomadic peoples who live by herding cattle, sheep, goats and—in the more desert areas—camels. The

Using an ox-drawn plough in the rich soil of the west

highlands with their abundant rainfall are the home of peasant farmers who till the land, in most cases with ox-drawn ploughs.

Industry is represented in Ethiopia by a number of cotton, sugar, tobacco, cement, brick, corrugated iron, shoe and other factories. These are mainly located in or around Addis Ababa and Asmara, and—to a lesser extent—Dire Dawa and Bahr Dar. Though the vast majority of the population still live in the countryside there are now at least two million town-dwellers, most of them in Addis Ababa.

A nomadic cattle herder

Some Glimpses of Life in Town and Country

Because of its immense geographical contrasts and its unique history, Ethiopia abounds in interesting sights which have long fascinated travellers from foreign parts.

Addis Ababa is today one of Africa's largest cities, with a population of well over a million inhabitants. It is, like the country itself, a place of many contrasts. As the capital of one of the most important countries on the continent, and the headquarters of several African and other international organisations, it is a major diplomatic centre, with many foreign embassies from all over the world. The city has a number of sky-scrapers and other modern buildings made of cement, stone and brick, including international-style hotels and restaurants, and brightly-lit shops, as well as fast-moving traffic.

On the other hand, Addis Ababa also has its more traditional side, with numerous rustic houses and bungalows. These are made of wooden poles and splintered lengths of wood which are plastered over with mud and then whitewashed. The roofs of such houses are usually made of corrugated iron. This has largely replaced the thatch of former times, although thatched houses are still common in the countryside. Most houses are set in compounds. These often contain a smaller dwelling in which the family's servant or servants sleep. Cooking is often done on a charcoal fire, and involves a considerable amount of smoke, as well as the smell of strong spices. It is therefore usually carried out in a kitchen some distance from the main dwelling, sometimes in a special shed in the compound. Many householders keep a cow, several sheep or perhaps a dozen or so chickens in the compound; and in recent years bee-keeping has become more widespread, with the result that these days people may have two or three beehives in their garden. It is not uncommon—particularly before Easter, which is a time of great festivity—to see herds of cattle, sheep and goats, as well as numerous chickens, being brought to the capital. The animals are purchased by the citizens of Addis Ababa, who will in many cases kill them at home—

The modern City Hall in Addis Ababa

Thatched houses in Lalibala

although the city is not without slaughter-houses and butchers' shops.

Ethiopian food consists in the main of a peppery and highly spiced stew called *wot* and a pancake-like bread called *enjara*. Ethiopians use the latter to pick up their food. Like many other peoples of Africa and the East, they almost invariably eat with their hands, and make very little use of cutlery. An Ethiopian wit called Alemayehu Mogus once visited Europe where he was asked whether it was true that his compatriots ate with their hands, whereupon he replied, "What! Do you have people in your country who eat with their feet?" Perhaps the country's greatest delicacy, which is mainly reserved for

31

banquets and special occasions, is raw meat. It is served highly spiced, either in large chunks or finely shredded like mince-meat.

Ethiopian housewives, many of whom pride themselves on special secret recipes which only they know, spend much of their time cooking. This tends to be laborious work, involving much cutting up of meat, and onions and other vegetables, and the grinding of all sorts of spices. Only a few town-dwellers include canned or packaged foods in their diet. Besides baking

A housewife preparing *wot*

their own bread, Ethiopian housewives prepare a home-made beer called *talla*, and hydromel or honey-wine, called *taj*. They also cut up pieces of raw meat which will be salted and spiced, and then hung up to dry. This makes a tasty dried food called *kwanta* which can be kept for months on end without going bad. A visitor to Addis Ababa, or indeed almost anywhere else in Ethiopia, can expect to see big flat baskets of red peppers and other spices drying in the sunshine, before being ground into powder to produce Ethiopia's most popular condiment. Called *barbare*, it is a mixture of red pepper and other spices, and is the basis of most of the country's tastiest stews.

Although there are, of course, many modern laundries in Addis Ababa, a large proportion of its inhabitants still wash their clothes in the city's several small streams, and then spread them out on the river banks to dry in the sun. This practice is even more general in the country at large, where (instead of using soap) people wash their clothes with the seeds of a plant called *endod*. It is amazing how dazzlingly clean and white these clothes become without the help of soap or modern detergents!

Many of Addis Ababa's inhabitants nowadays dress in European-type clothing. This is more or less universal in Government offices, as well as among the menfolk in general; though many women cling to the country's national dress which is also widely worn, by both men and women, on important holidays.

The traditional clothing of Ethiopian highlanders is made

People in the market in Addis Ababa

almost entirely of white cotton. Men wear white shirts and
trousers, and women white dresses. The clothes of the wealthy
are often finely embroidered with coloured silk. Both men and
women also wear a thin and delicate white wrap, the ends of
which are generally decorated with brightly-coloured stripes.
It is called a *shamma*, and is draped around the body with great
dignity, like the toga of the ancient Romans. When travelling
in the countryside, Ethiopian mountain people often wear
thick burnouses, or hooded capes, made of black sheep's wool.
These cloaks are almost rain-proof, and keep the wearer warm
even in the coldest weather. Many other types of clothes are
worn in different parts of the country. For example, the people
of the old walled city of Harar make use of brightly-coloured
cotton clothing, while some of the countryfolk south of Addis

34

Ababa have clothes made of leather which the women brighten up with coloured beads and bangles. Shepherd-boys, who watch their cattle day in and day out whatever the weather, also sometimes weave themselves coverings of straw which provide protection from the rain.

Despite the development of cotton factories after the Second World War in Addis Ababa, Dire Dawa and Bahr Dar, age-old methods of spinning and weaving are still practised in the more remote countryside. As in other parts of the world in former days, spinning is a women's occupation, while weaving is men's work. Spinning is carried out with a locally-made wooden roller or iron rod; and weaving with a simple wooden loom, in most cases made by the weaver himself. It is attached to stakes stuck in the ground, and enables the weaver to work in the open air.

Ethiopian weavers

Visitors to Ethiopia are invariably impressed by its beautiful jewellery, made of gold and silver as well as various cheap alloys. The gold, which is mined in the country, is of a rich reddish colour, and is almost pure. The silver is mainly obtained by melting down Maria Theresa dollars—old Austrian coins which circulated unofficially in Ethiopia in the eighteenth, nineteenth and early twentieth centuries. Ethiopian jewellers, who make use of only the simplest tools, nevertheless turn out ornate and very decorative work, including delicate filigree.

Ethiopia's finest jewellery, some of the best of which is made by jewellers from the ancient city of Aksum, includes crosses of all shapes and sizes, both for use in church and to be worn round the neck—a very common practice throughout the Christian areas of the country. Jewellers also produce an almost infinite variety of necklaces, lockets, hairpins, earrings, bracelets and even anklets, as well as little ear-picks or spoons which are used to clean the wax out of the ear. Jewellers in the old days also produced all kinds of ornaments for shields, swords, spears and even guns, as well as decorations for horses and mules. (The Ethiopians have always been great horsemen but, because of the rugged terrain, they tend to prefer the mule to the horse.) These ornaments can still be bought in Addis Ababa market.

Many other handicrafts are also practised, including basket-weaving and pottery. Basket-making is carried out entirely by women; they produce beautiful baskets of all shapes and

36

A filigree cross

colours. The finest are said to come from Harar. Baskets are extensively used as containers for many kinds of foods, both solid and liquid, for the Ethiopians know how to make their baskets entirely watertight when necessary. The *masob*, or table at which people eat, is likewise made of basketware, and is a familiar sight in every home.

Pottery, also made mainly by women, is in widespread use, particularly in the countryside. Ethiopian pottery is usually produced from red clay which becomes a rich shiny black when fired. Earthenware is used for cooking and—of import-

Basket-making at Bahr Dar

ance in every home—for brewing coffee, as well as for food receptacles of many kinds: jars, dishes and bowls of various sizes. The Ethiopians also use pottery to make the *gulelat,* or centre-piece, which they place as a decoration at the top of the thatched roofs of their round huts.

Ethiopians have long been skilled in the working of iron which is smelted from iron-ore found in small quantities in many parts of the country. Blacksmiths used to be much looked down upon by the rest of the population. Superstitious people even thought that workers in iron practised magic and turned themselves into hyenas at night, but early in the twentieth century Emperor Menilek insisted that blacksmiths should be recognised as of equal status to any other Ethiopian. In fact, as he realised, they played an essential role both in peace and war; for they make not only ploughshares and the iron parts of sickles and other agricultural implements, but also spear-heads and sword-blades, not to mention bits and stirrups for horses and mules. Blacksmiths still practise their craft in Ethiopia today, although factory-made ironware is increasingly coming into general use.

Until modern times Ethiopian artists, who were invariably attached to churches and monasteries, also played an important role in the country's life. They illustrated manuscript

Children carrying earthenware pots

copies of the Bible and other religious books (which were written on parchment) and painted icons, or sacred paintings on wood, as well as decorating the interior walls and ceilings of churches throughout the land. Old-style Ethiopian art, which is largely religious, is still being produced today and is much sought after by tourists. For the most part scenes are drawn from the Bible and other religious texts. Paintings are based on custom and convention, with little or no attempt at realism. One of the results of this is that there is usually no indication of perspective. Persons or objects are not made to

A religious painting, in traditional style

appear larger if they are close to the viewer, or smaller if they are far away. On the contrary, their size depends on their importance: a king will therefore be drawn large and a servant small, irrespective of where they may in fact be standing. Similarly, the various parts of the body are often not drawn to scale; a finger may be shown as long as an arm; and an eye, because of its importance, may be drawn considerably larger than life.

Another convention of Ethiopian art is that Christians (and good people in general) are depicted in full face, with two eyes, while evil people and enemies of the faith are shown in profile, with only a single eye. In battle scenes, it is normal practice for Ethiopians, and the righteous, to be placed on the left of the painting, and their enemies on the right.

The Ethiopians are keen on sport, and have a number of long-established games which are still frequently played in the countryside. Around Christmas-time it is the custom to play a type of hockey, called *ganna*. The boys and grown men of a village divide themselves into two teams, and play for hours on end with a ball made out of a rounded piece of wood which they hit with curved sticks cut from branches found in nearby forests. Another game, called *guks*, is a kind of mock-warfare played by two teams on horseback. The contestants each have three thin wands which they hurl like spears at their enemies, who ward them off with shields, as in the real warfare of bygone days.

Guks: a form of medieval jousting

Another game which was formerly very popular among the Ethiopian nobility was Ethiopian chess. This game is played with the same pieces and board as European chess, but with different rules. The Queen in the Ethiopian game can move, like the King, only one square at a time; Bishops, like Knights, are able to jump over intervening pieces. Another difference is that the two players are at first entitled to move *simultaneously*—they thus begin by moving their pieces forwards and backwards as fast as they can, to establish themselves in the

42

best possible position before the main contest starts. When the first capture takes place the rules change, and the players thenceforth move *alternately* as in the European game. Ethiopian chess is, however, now seldom played. Today, most Ethiopian chess-players have adopted the rules of the European form of the game.

Ethiopian children (including shepherd-boys) in the countryside often play a board-game known as *gabata*, variants of which are found in many parts of Africa. It is usually played by digging two rows of holes in the ground, or using a specially carved wooden board. Each row normally consists of six holes, each of which is initially filled with four pebbles or small stones. The players, who operate alternately, pick up the contents of one of the holes in the row nearest them, and then,

A traditional style painting of two people playing gabata

moving always in an anti-clockwise direction, drop the pebbles one by one into adjacent holes. On dropping the last pebble in their hand they pick up those in the hole in which it fell, and continue in this way until they reach an empty hole, or until they achieve a capture. This is done by increasing the contents of a hole from three to four pebbles. Games of this kind are sometimes played from early morning until late at night.

Youngsters in the towns have, on the whole, abandoned such old-style country games, and are turning more to Western-type football. Addis Ababa, Asmara and other cities have large stadiums where matches are played between pro-fessional and semi-professional teams. Ethiopian football-fans, who eagerly watch the World-Cup on television (brought to them by satellite), are ecstatic when the Africa-Cup is played in Addis Ababa.

Early Ethiopian History

Ethiopian history begins perhaps five hundred years before the birth of Christ, with the emergence of a major civilisation on the northern Horn of Africa.

The most lasting achievement of this civilisation was the creation of the Ge'ez, or Ethiopic, writing. This was one of the very few forms of writing ever developed on the African continent. With minor modifications, it is still used in Ethiopia to this day. The Ge'ez writing was derived from that of the Sabaeans of South Arabia who spoke a Semitic language. The Sabaean script, like that of most Semitic languages, consisted almost entirely of consonants, and made little use of vowels. It was written, again like the majority of Semitic languages,

ሀ	ha	ሁ	hu	ሂ	hi	ሃ	$h\bar{a}$	ሄ	$h\bar{e}$	ህ	$h, h\breve{u}, h\breve{e}$	ሆ	ho
ለ	la	ሉ	lu	ሊ	li	ላ	$l\bar{a}$	ሌ	$l\bar{e}$	ል	$l, l\breve{u}, l\breve{e}$	ሎ	lo
ሐ	$\d{h}a$	ሑ	$\d{h}u$	ሒ	$\d{h}i$	ሓ	$\d{h}\bar{a}$	ሔ	$\d{h}\bar{e}$	ሕ	$\d{h}, \d{h}\breve{u}, \d{h}\breve{e}$	ሖ	$\d{h}o$
መ	ma	ሙ	mu	ሚ	mi	ማ	$m\bar{a}$	ሜ	$m\bar{e}$	ም	$m, m\breve{u}, m\breve{e}$	ሞ	mo
ሠ	sa	ሡ	su	ሢ	si	ሣ	$s\bar{a}$	ሤ	$s\bar{e}$	ሥ	$s, s\breve{u}, s\breve{e}$	ሦ	so
ረ	ra	ሩ	ru	ሪ	ri	ራ	$r\bar{a}$	ሬ	$r\bar{e}$	ር	$r, r\breve{u}, r\breve{e}$	ሮ	ro
ሰ	sa	ሱ	su	ሲ	si	ሳ	$s\bar{a}$	ሴ	$s\bar{e}$	ስ	$s, s\breve{u}, s\breve{e}$	ሶ	so
ሸ	$\check{s}a$	ሹ	$\check{s}u$	ሺ	$\check{s}i$	ሻ	$\check{s}\bar{a}$	ሼ	$\check{s}\bar{e}$	ሽ	$\check{s}, \check{s}\breve{u}, \check{s}\breve{e}$	ሾ	$\check{s}o$
ቀ	qa	ቁ	qu	ቂ	qi	ቃ	$q\bar{a}$	ቄ	$q\bar{e}$	ቅ	$q, q\breve{u}, q\breve{e}$	ቆ	qo

Part of the Amharic alphabet used today

45

either from right to left, or else in a "ploughwise" manner whereby the first line of any sentence was from right to left, the second from left to right, the third from right to left, and so on. In Ge'ez, however, vowel signs were added to each consonant, so that every symbol came to represent a syllable, no longer merely a consonant as had been the case in the Sabaean. Another innovation in Ge'ez script was that, unlike Sabaean, it was written consistently from left to right.

The first capital of the Ge'ez-speaking people seems to have been at Yeha, in what is now Tigray province. This settlement was later replaced by Aksum, a little further south. This was destined to become one of the greatest cities of its time. The Aksumite kingdom, called after its capital, became the most powerful state between the Roman empire and Persia. It was visited by envoys and travellers from many lands.

Aksum, and its principal port, Adulis, which lay on the Red Sea, were both major commercial centres. They dealt in the export of ivory, gold and slaves, as well as a wide variety of imports, including cotton cloth, glassware, raw metals and such manufactured goods as swords and axes. These came mainly from Egypt, from the rest of the Mediterranean world and from India.

The Aksumites produced their own currency, in gold, silver and bronze. This was probably initiated by King Aphilas of Aksum in the third century A.D. Some of these coins, which continued to be minted for almost a thousand years, bear inscriptions in Greek which was then the international language of the Red Sea and eastern Mediterranean region. Others were in the national language: Ge'ez.

The people of Aksum were also great builders. They erected impressive stone palaces and temples, as well as fine obelisks, or monumental pillars, each beautifully cut out of a single piece of stone. Most of the buildings are now in ruins, but several of the obelisks are still standing; the tallest is almost 21 metres (70 feet) high. (One of these obelisks was taken to Italy during the Italian fascist occupation. It now stands in

The largest standing obelisk at Aksum

Rome, opposite the headquarters of the United Nations Food and Agricultural Organisation.)

Ezana, one of the greatest of the Aksumite rulers, conducted a number of successful campaigns in the early fourth century, and described them in a series of stone inscriptions which were written in Sabaean, Ge'ez and Greek. In these texts he tells of his expeditions to several parts of the country, including low-land areas (where camels were the principal means of transport) and the lofty Samen mountains, as well as westwards to the confluence of the Blue and White Niles in what is now the Sudan.

Perhaps the most important event of Ezana's reign was, however, the Aksumite state's conversion to Christianity. This took place in around the year 330 A.D. The conversion was recorded not long afterwards by the Roman historian Rufinus.

A camel caravan in northern Ethiopia

He notes that Meropius, a Greek-speaking philosopher from Tyre, had gone on a sea voyage to India, and had taken with him two boys whom he was educating. The elder was named Frumentius, and the younger Aedesius. On the return journey the ship put in for water at a harbour on the Red Sea coast, but was seized as a reprisal against the Romans for a treaty which was said to have been broken. Meropius was killed in the fighting, but the two boys escaped, and were later found studying under a tree. They were brought to the king of Aksum who made Aedesius his cup-bearer, and Frumentius, whom he saw to be wise and prudent, his treasurer and secretary. Both youths came to be held in great honour and affection. Not long afterwards the king died, leaving his wife with an infant son. Before he died, the king gave the two youngsters permission to return home. But his widow begged them, with tears in her eyes, to remain with her, and share in the government until her son came of age. The two young men willingly agreed. Frumentius, in particular, soon began to play an influential role in state affairs.

Frumentius duly established a number of Christian churches. When the young heir to the throne eventually reached the age to govern it was decided that Aedesius should return home to Tyre. Frumentius, on the other hand, journeyed to Alexandria, in Egypt, where he informed the great Patriarch Athanasius of the work thus far accomplished for Christianity at Aksum. He begged the prelate to find a worthy man to send as bishop to look after the many Christians already living there. Athanasius, after listening to Frumentius' story, declared, "What other man shall we find in whom the Spirit of God is as in thee, who can accomplish such things?" Frumentius was accordingly sent back to Aksum, as its first Christian bishop, and there adopted the name Abba Salama, meaning "Father of Peace".

It seems that the Aksumite prince whom he had helped to educate, and must have duly converted to Christianity, was none other than King Ezana. Proof of this can be seen in the fact that Ezana's earliest inscriptions refer to the old pre-Christian gods, while his later ones testify to his new-found Christian faith. His first coins similarly bear the effigy of the sun and moon, while the later ones are stamped with the Cross of Christ.

The next important ruler of Aksum was King Kaleb. In 523 A.D. he undertook an expedition to South Arabia, to avenge the persecution of Christians there. One of the results of this expedition was that part of South Arabia was brought under Aksumite control and remained so until its occupation by the Persians half a century or so later.

This period was also notable for the arrival in Ethiopia of a number of devout Christians from Syria; the best-known of them are spoken of as the Nine Saints. They founded several monasteries in the north of the country which played an important role in the subsequent development and expansion of Ethiopian Christianity.

Although the Aksumites were Christians, they at first had

A coin of King Ezana of Aksum, c. 330–335 A.D.

close ties with Islam. When the Prophet Muhammad first began his religious teachings in Arabia his followers faced severe persecution there. He therefore told them to flee to Ethiopia which he called "a land of righteousness where no one is wronged". In A.D. 615 a first group of Muslims accordingly sailed across the Red Sea to find refuge with the Aksumite ruler King Armah. Others followed, and it was not long before they are said to have numbered one hundred and one. They included Muhammad's daughter Rockeya, and one of his later wives, Habibah (who was then his betrothed). The rulers of Arabia, who were not yet converted to Islam, sent messengers to King Armah, asking him to return the refugees. But, after examining them on their beliefs, he replied, "If you were to offer me a mountain of gold I would not give up these people who have taken refuge with me." After Islam gained accept-

51

ance in Arabia, Armah sent the refugees back with costly presents, as well as a fine dowry for the Prophet's betrothed. Muhammad is believed to have been greatly moved. On learning of Armah's subsequent death he prayed for his soul, and ordered his followers to "leave the Abyssinians in peace", thereby exempting them from the sufferings of the *jihad*, or Holy War.

A Medieval Christian Realm

The Aksumite kingdom began to decline round about A.D. 900. At this time another kingdom emerged much further south in Lasta. A new ruling dynasty, named the Zagwe, gained power there. Their capital was at Roha, which was later renamed Lalibala, after King Lalibala, the most notable ruler of this dynasty. He is believed to have built the majority of the town's twelve famous rock-hewn churches which have been said to rank among the wonders of the world. These churches, though remarkable to foreign eyes, are perhaps less noteworthy in Ethiopia, since rock-hewn churches are to be found in many parts of the country, notably in Tigray. Such churches are usually carved in one piece out of the solid rock. As at Lalibala, they are frequently connected to each other by tunnels.

The rule of the Zagwe dynasty came to an end around the

year 1270 when Lalibala's grandson, Na'akuto La'ab, abdicated in favour of Yekuno Amlak, a prince from the more southerly province of Shoa, who claimed descent from the Queen of Sheba and King Solomon of Israel. He established an entirely new dynasty, known to historians (on account of its supposed descent) as the Solomonic line.

This change of dynasty marked a turning-point in Ethiopian history. The centre of political power, for the next two hundred and fifty years, was firmly established in Shoa, and the influence and wealth of the Church, which had supported Yekuno Amlak in his assumption of power, was greatly strengthened. The Church now became a major owner of land.

If Yekuno Amlak was the founder of the new dynasty, his grandson Emperor Amda Seyon (who ruled from 1314 to 1344) was the founder of its might and power. He carried out a series of campaigns which consolidated his control throughout central Ethiopia, and led to the creation of a powerful state. It was further strengthened by his great-grandson Zara Yaqob, who reigned from 1434 to 1468, and was perhaps the greatest ruler of Ethiopia since Ezana. Besides achieving further important military successes, he carried out a number of major administrative and religious reforms. He crushed the provincial rulers, strengthened the power and prestige of the monarchy, and suppressed what he regarded as Pagan or Jewish practices. He instituted a ruthless inquisition and a fierce persecution designed to destroy any kind of opposition to his rule. Even members of his own family were made to

suffer: he had his wife put to death, and he imprisoned his son
for mourning the death of his own mother.

The period after the establishment of the Solomonic dynasty
witnessed a flowering of Ethiopian literature. Many notable
literary works were produced, among them the *Fetha Nagast*,
or Laws of the Kings—the country's principal legal code; the
Kebra Nagast, or Glory of Kings, which told the legendary
story of the Queen of Sheba's visit to King Solomon; and the
Ethiopian royal chronicles, which contained a detailed
account of the reigns of the country's rulers. In some ways,
however, Ethiopia was now less advanced than in Aksumite

54

times. Building techniques, for example, had greatly deteriorated, perhaps because the monarchs of this period were constantly travelling from place to place, and had no fixed capital. There was, moreover, less foreign trade, and coins were no longer minted. People bartered for goods with blocks of salt or pieces of cloth instead of money.

Ethiopia nevertheless remained in contact with other lands. Each year, many Ethiopian Christians made pilgrimages to Jerusalem, where Sultan Saladin of Egypt and Syria had (in the twelfth century) given them permission to own a chapel. A smaller number of Ethiopians also visited Rome where (in the fourteenth century) the Pope allocated them a house. Several Ethiopian emperors were likewise in communication with foreign rulers. Early in the fifteenth century Emperor Dawit despatched an embassy to Egypt, with twenty camel-

Abba Libanos church, Lalibala

A priest with a
church treasure

loads of gifts. Later, in 1424, Emperor Yeshaq wrote to the King of Spain proposing an alliance and asking him to send him skilled workers. This appeal for craftsmen was echoed by a number of later rulers.

The Ethiopian state suffered a severe blow in 1527 when Ahmad Gragn (the Muslim ruler of Harar in the east of the country) rebelled, and proclaimed a Holy War against the Christians. Having acquired many firearms, which were then still little-known in this part of Africa, he defeated the Emperor, Lebna Dengel, and overran most of the country. Ahmad Gragn and his soldiers burnt down many churches, and caused much destruction. They were eventually defeated, in 1543, by Lebna Dengel's successor, named Galawdewos, who was assisted by a small but well-armed band of 400 Portuguese led by Christopher da Gama, the son of the famous explorer.

After the defeat of Gragn the country was much poorer than in pre-war days. Many men, women and children had been sold into slavery in Arabia, and large numbers of cattle had been killed. Another outcome of the fighting, and of the weakening of both Christians and Muslims, was that the Gallas, also known as Oromos, who inhabited the southern provinces began to advance northwards into what had, until then, been the heart of the empire. Shoa, which had formerly been more or less the centre of the realm, was largely abandoned by the rulers of the country. The capitals of the late sixteenth and early seventeenth century were all in the Lake Tana area of the north-west. Another problem was created at about the same time when the Turks, who had been expanding along the Red Sea coast, succeeded in 1557 in seizing the port of Massawa. This effectively blocked Ethiopia's access to the sea.

Two emperors, Za Dengel and later Susenyos, adopted the Catholic faith in the hope that this would help them in obtaining assistance from Portugal as a Catholic country. Acting on the advice of Jesuit missionaries, Susenyos also tried to persuade his subjects to embrace Catholicism, but most of them refused to abandon their old faith. He then attempted to achieve their conversion by force but this merely provoked a rebellion. Realising that his efforts were futile he issued a proclamation restoring the Ethiopian orthodox religion. He then abdicated, in 1632, in favour of his son Fasiladas who immediately expelled the Jesuits. These events were welcomed with great popular enthusiasm. Many Ethiopians, it is said, danced with joy, and broke to pieces all the Catholic rosaries they could find. The new emperor then proclaimed that henceforward no more Catholics should be allowed in the land.

Not long after this, in 1636, Fasiladas established his capital at Gondar. This was the first important capital of the country for many centuries. Fasiladas gave orders for the building of a castle which was designed by an Indian architect, and which can be seen to this day. Several later emperors also erected

Some of the castles in Gondar

castles with the result that the city—which was by then an important political, economic and religious capital—became by far the finest in the country, with a population of perhaps 100,000 inhabitants.

In the middle of the eighteenth century the Ethiopian state faced new difficulties. The powers of the monarchs declined, the principal provinces became more or less independent of each other, and there was much fighting between regional rulers. Commerce suffered greatly, although—because of unsettled conditions—the slave trade continued to flourish. One of the many Ethiopians torn from his family and sold abroad as a slave, early in the eighteenth century, was a certain Abraham who was taken by way of Constantinople to Russia: his great-grandson was the famous Russian poet Alexander Pushkin (1789-1837).

Preserving National Independence

At the beginning of the nineteenth century, Ethiopia was a disunited land, torn by civil war. Because of industrial developments in other countries, it was steadily falling behind Europe and even Egypt. Three notable Ethiopian rulers attempted successively to unify the country, and to undertake its modernisation.

The first was Emperor Tewodros, or Theodore, who has been called one of the most remarkable men of nineteenth-century Africa. He started his political career as a chief named Kassa, in Qwara, a district on the borders of the Sudan. He then fought his way to power, and was duly crowned Emperor in 1855. He chose the name Tewodros, on account of a legend, then widely believed, which prophesied that a monarch of that name would appear who would rule justly, defeat Islam, and capture Jerusalem.

His objective, on becoming emperor, was to reunite the country, and to begin the task of its modernisation. He undertook military expeditions to the various provinces to bring them under his control. He also reorganised his army, established taxes for its maintenance, and ordered the soldiers not to steal from the peasants as they had done formerly. To strengthen his army he used the technical skills of Protestant missionaries to cast cannons and mortars. Also with the help of the missionaries, he built the first roads in his country. He wisely planned to send Ethiopians abroad to learn how to make guns. Tewodros failed, however, to achieve most of his ambitions. This was because his reign was disturbed by much fighting. The provincial chiefs opposed his policy of unification, and were strongly supported by the Church which disliked his plans for reform.

Tewodros tried, in the 1860s, to obtain craftsmen from Britain to make guns and undertake other skilled work. He wrote to Queen Victoria about this, but received no reply. A quarrel therefore developed between him and the British government, as a result of which he imprisoned the British Consul and other foreigners, including several missionaries, at his court. The British government retaliated by despatching a military expedition against him. It was led by Sir Robert Napier who landed at the Red Sea port of Zulla on October 21, 1867, crossed Tigray without any opposition from its local rulers, and reached Tewodros's mountain fortress of Magdala in April of the following year. The first fighting between Tewodros and the British took place on April 10, 1868, and was resumed two days later.

The Ethiopians were defeated by the invaders' superior fire-power. Rather than face capture, Tewodros shot himself in the mouth with a pistol, just as the British troops rushed into his fortress on April 13. The British then set fire to Magdala, and carried away about one thousand valuable Ethiopian

This painting, from an Ethiopian manuscript looted from Magdala and now in London's British Library, shows a church being hewn from solid rock at Lalibala

manuscripts. Nearly half of these were taken to London, where they can still be seen in the British Library.

The Emperor Tewodros' death brought a sudden end to all his ambitious plans. There followed a fierce struggle for power between various contenders for the throne.

The next important nineteenth-century ruler was Emperor Yohannes, or John, a chief from Tigray. His rise to power owed much to the British who had given him a large gift of arms in 1868, as a reward for his neutrality during the Magdala campaign.

Despite his failure to oppose the British, Yohannes was a keen patriot, as well as a devout supporter of the Ethiopian

62

orthodox church. He was also the first ruler of his country for several centuries to achieve decisive victories over major foreign enemies. The Egyptians, who were then well armed, and had been trained by European and American officers, invaded his country in the 1870s, but he defeated them at the battles of Gundet and Gura, in November 1875 and March 1876 respectively. Later, in February 1885, the Italians, who were just beginning to think of establishing a colonial empire, seized the port of Massawa. They began to advance inland, but were defeated by Ras Alula, the Emperor Yohannes' heroic commander of the north, at the battle of Dogali, in January 1887.

In the last two years of his reign Yohannes was troubled by attacks from the Sudan, then under the control of the fanatical Mahdists. The Mahdists, also known as Dervishes, invaded

Massawa, the oldest of Ethiopia's ports, as it is today

Gojjam and Bagemder. At this time also the Italians were planning another advance inland from Massawa. Yohannes succeeded in defeating the Dervishes at the battle of Matamma in March 1889, but was killed by a sniper's bullet fired by one of the enemy. His army fled the field of battle when they saw their leader was dead. The Italians meanwhile took advantage of the Emperor Yohannes' death, and of a serious famine which had then broken out, to advance again from Massawa. In 1890, they established their Red Sea colony of Eritrea.

Menilek, the third of the three great nineteenth-century rulers of Ethiopia, was a prince of Shoa whom Emperor Tewodros had captured on one of his expeditions to that province. He had kept him in detention at Magdala, with other nobles, but Menilek had escaped, in 1865, and proclaimed himself king of

Shoa. From the outset of his career he was inspired by Tewodros' dream of unifying and modernising Ethiopia. He sought to strengthen his army by befriending the European powers and importing sizeable quantities of firearms.

On the death of Yohannes, Menilek proclaimed himself emperor. To gain international recognition he signed a Treaty of Perpetual Peace and Friendship with the Italian government at the village of Wuchale on May 2, 1889. The Wuchale Treaty, as it is generally known, was written in Amharic and Italian, and contained clauses of benefit to both parties. However, a dispute soon broke out about one of the clauses: Article XVII. Its Amharic text stated that Menilek *could* use the services of the Italians for all communications he might wish to make with other countries, but the Italian version said that he *must* do so.

**An engraving of
Emperor Menilek II**

The Italians used this latter text to claim that the agreement had given them a protectorate over Ethiopia. Menilek, however, rejected this claim. To the King of Italy he wrote, "When I made the treaty . . . I said that because of our friendship, our affairs in Europe might be carried out by the sovereign of Italy, but I have not made any treaty which obliges me to do so." Not long afterwards, in February 1890, he wrote to the Great Powers, informing them that he did not accept the Italian interpretation of the agreement, and proudly declared, "Ethiopia has need of no one; she stretches out her hands to God."

The Italians meanwhile had been steadily occupying northern Tigray. Menilek, who had been actively importing arms, marched north to meet them. The first engagement took place in January 1895, but the decisive battle was not fought until March of the following year when the two armies clashed at Adwa. Menilek, who had forty cannon and 100,000 rifles against the Italians' fifty-six cannon and 14,500 rifles, was completely victorious. The invaders were routed, and they left behind them most of their weapons. Shortly after the battle the Italians abandoned their claim to a protectorate, and they and all the European powers recognised Ethiopia's status as an independent state. Menilek, whose international prestige had been greatly enhanced by his victory, shortly afterwards received diplomatic missions from the principal powers of the day. These included Britain, France, Italy, Russia, Germany, Austria, Belgium and the United States, most of whom established legations at his capital within the next few years. Despite

66

An Ethiopian painting of the Battle of Adwa

his great victory, Menilek was unable to drive the Italians out of their colony of Eritrea. This they retained.

Menilek's importance lies not only in that he maintained his country's independence in the face of the Italian threat, but also that he was the founder of the modern Ethiopian state. He was always interested in new inventions, and displayed an almost childlike fascination with new equipment. One Italian observer commented that if a builder of castles in the air came to Ethiopia with a plan to construct an escalator from the earth to the moon Menilek would have asked him to build it, "if only to see whether it could be done".

Perhaps Menilek's most notable achievement was the founding, in 1885–1886, of a new capital to which his consort, Queen Taytu, gave the name of Addis Ababa. He was also responsible for many modern innovations of all kinds. These included the

The city of Addis Ababa today

introduction of the country's first national currency and post-age stamps, in 1894, and the granting in the same year of a concession for the railway between Addis Ababa and Jibuti. The construction began in 1897, and reached the mid-way station of Dire Dawa in 1902.

In the 1890s Menilek sent the first Ethiopian students abroad to study in Switzerland and in Russia. He encouraged French and Italian engineers to establish a telegraph service, arranged for the Russian Red Cross to open Addis Ababa's first hospital, and sponsored the introduction into Ethiopia (from Australia) of the fast-growing eucalyptus tree or blue gum.

Later, in the early twentieth century, he began work on Ethiopia's first modern road, which led westwards from Addis Ababa. He also founded a number of new institutions, includ-

68

ing a mint in 1902, the Bank of Abyssinia (the country's first bank) in 1905, the Menilek School (the first modern educational establishment) in 1908, the Menilek Hospital (the first government hospital) in 1910, and the first state printing press in 1911.

All these developments were achieved with foreign help, but Menilek took care not to obtain assistance from any one source. He used French, British and Italian capital and skill, without falling under the influence of any single European power.

Menilek's right to be considered the founder of modern Ethiopia also rests on the fact that he rebuilt the greatness of the country, in the last quarter of the nineteenth century, by re-asserting control over the southern provinces which had been lost at the time of Ahmad Gragn's invasion in the early sixteenth century. He was thus responsible for establishing most of Ethiopia's present-day frontiers.

The last years of his reign were, however, a period of renewed difficulty. In December 1906 the three neighbouring colonial powers—Britain, France and Italy—anticipating his approaching death, and the break-up of his realm, came together to sign a Tripartite Treaty which divided the country between them into three spheres of economic influence. Menilek, however, commented that the treaty could not in any way bind his actions. In the following year, realising that his powers were failing, he established the country's first cabinet, with ministers appointed for various branches of government business.

In the years which followed, the old ruler's health steadily declined. He eventually died in December 1913. His grandson, Lej Iyasu, who took over the government, tried to win the support of the Muslim population, but this had the result of alienating the nobility of Shoa, and with it the Church. He also made the mistake, during the First World War, of befriending the Germans, Austrians and Turks. As a result he lost the support of the Allied powers—Italy, France and Britain. A rebellion against his rule soon broke out in Shoa, and he was defeated in 1916. After this it was decided that Menilik's daughter, Zawditu, should become Empress, and that Tafari, the son of the old Emperor's cousin Ras Makonnen, should be Regent and heir to the throne.

As a result of this arrangement stability was re-established, despite underlying rivalry between the Empress and Regent. The work of modernisation begun by Menilek was resumed. Regent Tafari brought Ethiopia into the League of Nations in 1923, and the first of several decrees for the gradual suppression of slavery was issued in the following year.

During the next few years the Regent established a new school and a new hospital in the capital, concluded a treaty of friendship with Italy, sent large numbers of students abroad, and introduced, in 1929, the first aeroplanes. In the previous year, 1928, Tafari had been given the rank of King. This replaced his earlier title of Ras, and gave him some inter-national fame. An interesting consequence of this was the founding (far away in the West Indies) of the Ras Tafarian movement, so-named by students of the Bible who saw his coronation as a confirmation of the Biblical prophecy that "Princes shall come out of Egypt". This movement later gained considerable strength. Its supporters, who keenly identify themselves with Ethiopia, are today found not only in the West Indies, but also in the United States and, as a result of West Indian immigration, also in Britain. Ras Tafarians may thus be seen sporting the colours of the Ethiopian flag— green, yellow and red—in London, New York, Washington and other major cities of the Western world. Ras Tafarians are, however, seldom seen in Ethiopia itself, for the movement made no converts in the country of its spiritual origin.

On Empress Zawditu's death, in 1930, Tafari Makonnen assumed the throne as Emperor Haile Selassie. Modernisation

Emperor Haile Selassie

Addis Ababa: Parliament

was accelerated, with the founding of a number of provincial
and other schools and hospitals, including the first school for
girls, the building of several major roads, and the establishment of the first radio station, as well as the nationalisation
of the Bank of Abyssinia, the setting up of a Government
printing press, and the despatch of increasing numbers of
students abroad. Other developments included a second
decree for the abolition of slavery, the founding of a military
college (run by Swedes), and the opening of the country's
first parliament. However, the members of parliament were
not elected but chosen by the Emperor.

72

Invasion, Liberation and Revolution

Although he had concluded a treaty of friendship with Ethiopia in 1928, the Italian fascist dictator, Benito Mussolini, determined a few years later to seize the country, and to expand the nearby Italian colonies of Eritrea and Somalia into an Italian East African empire. In 1932, therefore, he despatched one of his ministers, General De Bono, to Eritrea with orders that "the matter must be settled not later than 1936".

Italian troops from Somalia were meanwhile penetrating into the Ethiopian province of Ogaden where the frontier was not clearly marked. On November 23, 1934, they clashed with an Ethiopian force at Walwal, a post one hundred kilometres (sixty-two miles) inside Ethiopian territory. The Ethiopians resisted, but were driven back by Italian aircraft and tanks. Mussolini then demanded that Ethiopia should apologise for the incident, pay compensation, and recognise Walwal as being within Italian colonial territory. Emperor Haile Selassie refused, whereupon Mussolini declared that he would avenge the Italian defeat at Adwa in 1896, that Italy needed its "place in the sun", and that he planned to settle large numbers of Italians as colonists in Ethiopia.

The British and French, the two main powers in the area, declared themselves neutral, and announced that they would not supply arms to either side. Since Italy manufactured its own weapons, whereas Ethiopia had to import them from abroad, this decision in fact only affected Ethiopia, and directly helped Italy.

Italian forces started to invade, without any declaration of war, on October 3, 1935. The League of Nations, which had been established a generation earlier to prevent war, found Italy guilty of aggression, but decided only on a policy of economic sanctions against the invader. This meant that member states were asked to stop trading with Italy or lending her money. Petrol, however, was excluded from the list of prohibited supplies. This omission was a serious one, for Italy had to import all its petrol from abroad, and without petrol supplies the Italian army and air-force would not have been able to move.

The Italians meanwhile were steadily advancing into Ethiopia. They made effective use of artillery, tanks and planes, and—at critical moments—of poison-gas. They also bombed foreign Red Cross hospitals in the hope of driving away foreigners who would otherwise observe the methods of war Italy was employing. Hopes that the League of Nations might take more effective steps to halt the invasion were dashed in December when the British and French Foreign Ministers, Samuel Hoare and Pierre Laval, produced a compromise plan which would have allowed Italy outright control of half of Ethiopia as well as economic rights in the rest of the country.

74

While these and other talks proceeded the Italians continued their advance. They defeated the Emperor's army after fierce fighting at May Chaw on March 31, 1936. Haile Selassie left Addis Ababa on May 2 for Europe where he addressed the League of Nations in Geneva before going into exile in Britain. Three days after his departure from Addis Ababa Italian troops occupied the city. The League of Nations then abandoned sanctions, and most foreign powers soon recognised the Italian conquest. The United States and the Soviet Union were two of the few powers who refused to do so.

Despite the collapse of organised resistance and the capture by the Italians of Addis Ababa and other towns, the invaders encountered vigorous opposition in the countryside. Ethiopian patriot leaders, among them Ababa Aragay, Geresu Duke and Balay Zalaka, rallied together bands of warriors who fought as guerrillas. This resistance was particularly effective in Gojjam, Bagemder and Shoa. An attempt by two Eritreans, on the life of the Italian viceroy, General Graziani, in Addis Ababa in February 1937 was followed by swift and ferocious retaliation in which several thousand Ethiopians, including a good proportion of the educated population, were deliberately killed in a three-day massacre. Because of his inability to crush the patriots, Graziani was later replaced as Viceroy by an Italian nobleman, the Duke of Aosta, who adopted a somewhat more liberal policy in the hope of reducing popular resistance. The patriots, however, continued their operations, immobilising large Italian armies.

The Italians meanwhile were spending vast sums on their newly established empire. Immediate strategic interests and long-term economic considerations caused them to devote most of their efforts to road-building, as a result of which they established a road network throughout the empire. Other economic activity was, however, restricted. Trade stagnated, in part because the Italians expelled all foreign merchants, in part because they discouraged commerce by tight controls, and in part because they insisted on introducing Italian paper money which proved unacceptable to the Ethiopian peasants who were accustomed only to silver coins. Efforts were made to settle Italians on the land, but only slow progress was achieved, largely because of lack of funds. Racist policies were introduced to segregate the Ethiopian population. Those schools and

A winding road built by the Italians between Asmara and Massawa

After the defeat of the Italians, an Ethiopian soldier sings of his part in the victory

hospitals which were opened were mainly restricted to Europeans.

Mussolini's decision to enter the Second World War by declaring war on Britain and France in June 1940 brought about a sudden change in the Horn of Africa. The Ethiopian patriots, who had been fighting alone for four years, at last found themselves with allies, while the Italian troops found themselves isolated from their homeland. The British, anxious to destroy fascist power in East Africa, despatched two

77

officers, Brigadier Sandford and Colonel Wingate, to make contact with the patriots. In January 1941, British and other Allied forces launched a successful offensive against the Italians, from the Sudan into Eritrea and from Kenya into Italian Somalia. The Emperor, who had been flown from Britain for the purpose, crossed the frontier from the Sudan and, joining up with the patriots, advanced across Gojjam.

The Italian East African empire, which was being attacked by the Allies from without and by the patriots from within, then rapidly crumbled. Addis Ababa fell on April 6 to South African troops advancing from the south, and Haile Selassie returned to the capital on May 5, five years to the day after the entry of Mussolini's troops in 1936.

Relations between Britain and Ethiopia were cool in the years which followed, mainly because the British government tried to establish a virtual protectorate over the country, and insisted on remaining in occupation of wide stretches of it. The Emperor, however, gradually strengthened his position, and succeeded in regaining control of all Ethiopia's pre-1935 territory. He also developed increasingly close relations with the United States.

The late 1940s and early 1950s were a significant period of reconstruction. They witnessed the establishment of a new bank in 1942, a new currency in 1945, the first national air service—Ethiopian Airlines—in 1946, and the first institution of higher learning—the University College of Addis Ababa (the nucleus of a subsequent Haile Selassie I University)—

78

in 1950. Many schools, hospitals and other institutions were also opened, and the road system was reorganised.

No less important was the federation of the former Italian colony of Eritrea to Ethiopia. This took place as the result of a United Nations decision in 1952, and was followed by the complete integration of the territory ten years later. Ethiopia was by now in much closer contact with the outside world than in former times, and in particular was beginning to play a major role in inter-African politics. Addis Ababa was chosen as the headquarters of the United Nations' Economic Commission for Africa (E.C.A.) in 1958, and of the Organisation of African Unity (O.A.U.) in 1963.

Addis Ababa: Africa Hall

Opposition to Haile Selassie's long rule was by then growing. In December 1960, his bodyguard attempted to seize power. This move was easily crushed, but gained considerable support among University College and other students. In the years which followed, anti-government demonstrations became a regular occurrence. One of these protested against the government's alleged failure to deal with the 1972-4 famine in Tigray and Wallo. Later, in February 1974, a rise in the price of petrol resulted in a wave of strikes in Addis Ababa, accompanied by mutinies in the armed forces. This led to an unprecedented event: the resignation of the Emperor's government. The soldiers then began arresting former ministers and dignitaries, including Haile Selassie's closest associates and advisers. The Emperor himself was finally deposed on September 12. The old constitution, and parliament, were abolished, and a Provisional Military Administrative Council (P.M.A.C.) was established. Sixty former ministers and others were executed one night in November; and in December Ethiopia was proclaimed a socialist state.

Many far-reaching reforms were at once carried out. All rural and urban land and over one hundred companies were nationalised, students were sent into the countryside to assist with literacy and other programmes, and peasants', women's, and urban dwellers' associations were set up. These were to play a major rôle in the people's everyday life.

The collapse of the Emperor's rule, and dissatisfaction with the government's policies, led meanwhile to the rise of

An open-air literacy class in the country

splinter movements in many parts of the country—notably in Eritrea, the Afar country in the north-east, the Somali-inhabited Ogaden in the south-east, and some areas inhabited by Gallas or Oromos in the south. There was also strong opposition by landlords who had suffered from land national-isation—particularly in the north and north-west—as well as by students and others who objected to military government. All this led to much turmoil, and to civil war.

The Ethiopian Revolution faced a further major crisis in July 1977 when the government of neighbouring Somalia, which assumed that Ethiopia was on the verge of collapse, chose that moment to invade in the hope of annexing the Ethiopian Ogaden. The Somali army, which had been built up by the Soviet Union, succeeded in advancing to the gates of

Harar and Dire Dawa, but the Ethiopian air-force managed to retain control of the air. The Ethiopian armies, at first forced to retreat, eventually held their lines. Faced with the emergency the Ethiopian Government turned to the Soviet Union for help. The Soviet Union responded with a massive air-lift of men and supplies, and Russian and Cuban soldiers then collaborated with the Ethiopian army in driving out the Somali invaders. These events, not surprisingly, had major international repercussions, and caused Ethiopia which (before the Revolution) had been associated with the United States, to ally itself instead with the Soviet Union. Ethiopia, like Somalia before it, became officially committed to a Marxist philosophy.

The Gate of the Shah, in the wall of the old city of Harar

Ethiopia Today

Following its revolution, Ethiopia faces many difficulties. An old, and until 1974, largely tradition-bound society has in the last decade or so undergone many radical changes. Several large areas, including Tigray, Wallo and much of Hararge, have suffered moreover from several years of drought and famine. In addition, these and other regions, including Eritrea, have been impoverished by civil war. Political turmoil, as in other countries in the process of revolution, has been accompanied over the years by many arrests. The Somali invasion of the Ogaden in 1977–1978, and extensive purchase of arms for national defence, have also imposed a heavy burden on the country's entire economy. As a result of these arms purchases, and the increased costs of petrol and manufactured goods, Ethiopia is currently suffering an acute shortage of foreign exchange. Imported goods are in extremely limited supply, and the authorities have for many years been obliged to ration petrol. Several hundred thousand Ethiopians have for one reason or another fled the country, mainly to the Sudan and other neighbouring countries. Some have left in search of better employment opportunities, and this has increased Ethiopia's shortage of skilled workers.

The large number of Ethiopians now living outside their

native country constitute some of the largest expatriate communities of modern times. While the forty million Ethiopians living in their own native land face the immense problem of developing their ancient country, half a million or more of their brothers and sisters in other lands are facing the difficulty of adjusting to a new way of life. Besides the ordinary day-to-day problem of earning their living, these overseas Ethiopians are confronted with the question of how to preserve their Ethiopian identity, and to ensure that their children will not lose their language and culture. There is also the question of to what extent they and their descendants will continue to live abroad in the years and decades ahead and thus, almost inevitably, sever their links with their homeland— and to what extent they will decide to return home to assist in the vital task of Ethiopia's reconstruction.

Meanwhile, the Revolutionary Government has succeeded in keeping all the normal services—education, health, aviation, ports, telephones, etc.—in operation with scarcely any interruption. It has also made progress in eradicating feudal traditions, and carrying out land reform in a country in which this had hitherto seemed more or less impossible.

The establishment of peasants' and urban dwellers' associations may also prove of immense value in bridging the gap between government and people, and in making it possible for the Ethiopians to shape their own future. These associations also serve a useful purpose in the distribution of cost-price food and other articles in short supply. Much time is spent at association meetings discussing a variety of local issues. In government departments where things are arranged on a more formal basis, all employees are expected to gather each week to discuss political affairs, as well as to study Marxist texts.

The Government has also shown its determination to struggle against drought and famine. It has worked hard to mobilise international support for the relief projects which it has established throughout the land.

No less praiseworthy have been the Government's efforts to redress old injustices and inequalities. Official recognition has been given for the first time to Muslim as well as Christian holidays. Broadcasting and publishing have been carried out in Ethiopian languages other than Amharic. (The use of such languages was in former times actively discouraged). Women's

A peasant farmer reading a book printed in the Oromo (or Galla) language

associations have been established with the object of emancipating the female population.

The most impressive achievement of the post-revolutionary decade has, however, been the Literacy Campaign. This has been carried out with great vigour by the Government and the various local associations in all parts of the country—even in remote villages and among nomadic communities. Attendance at literacy classes was compulsory, and people with employees could be punished if they failed to ensure that the employees went to class. Every night in Addis Ababa and other towns vast crowds of women, draped in their traditional white *shammas*, or cotton wraps, can be seen walking to their classes. As a result, the literacy rate, which was little more than ten per cent on the eve of the Revolution, rose within only a few years to over fifty per cent. Illiteracy has been virtually abolished in all towns, where most houses now display little

Ethiopians wearing traditional dress

A water-hole in a semi-desert area of Ethiopia

red notices proclaiming that everyone within can read and write. Literacy, once the privilege of the few, has become the right of all.

Despite these and other changes, Ethiopia remains a poor and economically underdeveloped country. The vast majority of its forty million inhabitants still live in the countryside as simple peasant farmers or semi-nomadic herdsmen. Most men in the highlands still work the land as their ancestors did, with rustic wooden ploughs pulled by a couple of oxen. The womenfolk cook in locally-made clay pots over charcoal fires placed between stones set on the floor in the middle of their huts. The younger male members of the family spend most of the daylight hours looking after cattle, while girls remain with

87

የአዲስ አበባ መሠረት ትምህርት ዘመቻ
አስተባባሪና አስፈጻሚ ኮሚቴ
ጽሕፈት ቤት

ግይምነት በተግላችን ይወድግላ !

ከግይምነት መላቀቁን/ጹን / ያረጋገጡ
የመ /ት /ዘ /ሸ /ኤ /ኮ /አባላት

ሰም _____ ፊርማ
1. _____
2. _____
3. _____
4. _____

ይህ ግረጋገጫ
ከቦታው ቢነሳ በሕግ
የሚያስጠጣ መሆኑን
እናሳስባለን

ከፍተኛ _____
ተበሊ _____
የቤት ቁጥር _____

ከቤቴ ግዮም የሌላና ለወደፊቱም ቢገኝ ለግስተግር ቃል ገብቻለሁ ።

የቤተሰብ ኃላፊ ፊርማ _____

በእብዮታችን ከግይምነት ተላቀናል

A literacy certificate

their mothers in the house or, at certain seasons, weed the fields.

Similarly, conditions have changed little in the lowlands. Here entire families—men, women and children—live in the flimsiest of huts which are, in many cases, dismantable. They devote almost all their time to tending their livestock. Although the Literacy Campaign has made great strides, many children still do not go to school, and villages are without clinics or modern medical facilities of any kind.

Ethiopia today remains one of the world's poorest countries. If they are lucky, peasants, herdsmen and others produce each year only sufficient for that year's needs. If things go wrong, entire communities are faced by acute famine, as was the case during the early 1980s.

The country, like other parts of the Third World, also

88

suffers from the fact that the price of its farm produce and principal exports—in Ethiopia's case, mainly coffee—have in recent years been rising less steeply than those of its essential imports, particularly petrol and manufactured goods. The Ethiopian farmer has thus each year been obliged to toil in the fields harder and longer to pay for every piece of cotton clothing, as well as (if he can in fact afford one) perhaps his only luxury—a transistor radio.

Most Ethiopians are, nevertheless, accustomed to what Europeans or North Americans would consider immense deprivations. They accept them with fortitude, even with fatalism. Life for the average Ethiopian is moreover far from monotonous. It is enriched by frequent and very colourful religious and other ceremonies—numerous wedding celebrations, often held in tents, which the entire village or local

Picking coffee

community will attend; and, on the occasion of burials, huge
funeral banquets. Formal lunches and dinners are, in fact,
held on almost every possible occasion, and will be livened by
humorous conversation and witty replies.

As elsewhere, poverty in Ethiopia represents a major
obstacle to progress, for the country is too poor to afford
development projects which would make it rich. The Ethiopians are, however, fortunate to possess much good soil and
abundant rainfall. Their country could become the granary
of the Middle East. There are, moreover, sizeable mineral
resources awaiting exploitation—gold, platinum and, in all
probability, also oil.

The Ethiopians, despite their many current difficulties, can
look forward to the future with confidence. There is every hope
that their age-old country, which maintained its independence

90

throughout the era of the "Scramble for Africa", will be able to overcome the present-day problems of poverty and economic under-development, and that it will rank in the twenty-first century as one of the greatest and most honoured of African states.

Index

93

Rudolf, Lake 16
Rufinus 48
Russia 66, 68, 75, 81–2
Russians 82

Sabaean language 45–6, 48
Sabaeans 11, 45
Saho language 23
Saladin 55
Samen mountains 48
sanctions 9, 75
Sandford, Brigadier 78
schools 79
Scramble for Africa 7–8, 91
Second World War 10, 77
Semitic languages 20–1, 45–6
shamma 34
Sheba, Queen of 53–4
Shoa 53, 57, 64–5, 70, 75
slavery 57, 59, 72
slaves 46, 57, 59
Solomon 53–4
Solomonic dynasty 53–4
Somali language 23
Somalia 14, 16, 23, 73, 81
Somalis 81, 83
Spain 56
spices 32–3
spinning 35
sports 41–2, 44
Sudan 14, 24, 48, 60, 63, 78, 83
Susenyos 57
Swedes 72
Switzerland 68
Syria 50, 55
Syrians 24

Tafari Makonnen, Ras 70–1
taj 33
Takazee river 16
talla 33
Tana, Lake 57
tanks 73–4

Taytu 67
telegraph 68
Tewodros II 60–1, 64
Tigray 22, 46, 52, 62, 66, 80, 83
Tigre language 22
Tigrinya language 22
tourists 20, 40
Turks 57–8, 70
Tyre 49–50

U.S.S.R. 75, 81–2
United Nations 11, 79
United States of America 66, 71, 75, 78, 82
University College of Addis Ababa 78, 80

Victoria 61
villages 88

Wallo 80, 83
Walwal 73

Washington 71
weaving 35
Webi Shebeli river 16
West Indies 71
Wingate, Colonel 78
wot 31
written language 12
Wuchale treaty 65–6

Yeha 46
Yekuno Amlak 53
Yeshaq 56
Yohannes IV 62–5

Za Dengel 57
Zagwe dynasty 52
Zara Yaqob 53
Zawditu 70, 71
Zulla 61

95